i sing for my dead in german

i sing for my dead in german

Audrey Poetker

Turnstone Press

Published with the assistance of the Manitoba Arts Council and the Canada Council.

Turnstone Press
607 - 99 King Street
Winnipeg, Manitoba
Canada R3B 1H7

Typeset by: Communigraphics
Printed by: Hignell Printing Limited
for Turnstone Press

Printed in Canada.

Cover design: Roger Lusty.

Several of these poems have appeared in CV/2, *Herizons*, *Waves*, *Quarry*, *Wascana Review*, *Scrivener*, *The Dinosaur Review*, and *Border Crossings*.

Canadian Cataloguing in Publication Data

Poetker, Audrey, 1962-

I sing for my dead in German

Poems.
ISBN 0-88801-108-3

I. Title.

PS8581.04617 1986 C811'.54 C86-098018-9
PR9199.3.P6317 1986

for Susie,
Grosmama & Grospapa Wiebe,
& Grospapa Poetker

"I have fought a good fight,
I have finished my course,
I have kept the faith."

— II Timothy 4:7

CONTENTS

my grandfather is dead 1
knowing the mind works against breasts 2
Grandfather Poetker 4
the other woman 5
She Was Beautiful Then, Dancing 6
okay joe 7
The Adulterers: Trying to Say Love 8
The Rider 10
Gramma 12
A Friend Asks If He's Told Me He Loves Me 14
How to Have an Abortion 16
Fathers' Day Poem 17
215 21
everything here is a poem 22
The Notorious Other Woman 25
in the theatre 26
conversation 27
well dont you 28
Austria: Looking through the *National Geographic* 29
leaving 34
coma 36
in one fantasy you left your wife 38
Susie 40
A Poem for Michael: Lost in the Triangle 42
so you say you love me eh 45
alpha & omega 47
The National News Had No Flashback on Your Life 49
Laughter 51
what you see 52

The Night Is Thick & Black & Hot 53
Sisters 55
i had not meant not to play the game 57
call it what you want 59
this is an accident 61
& this is all 63
this is a blue animal youre reading about 64
touching home 65
sunday evening 67
Letter to Susie 70
Letter to Susie (ii) 72
Letter to Susie (iii) 74
essay (untitled) 79

i sing for my dead in german

my grandfather is dead
(in memory of Grandfather Poetker)

a fist pressed to my chest
   to keep
his blood from escaping to
   the grave
intricate letters worms form on
   his corpse
laughing bitter-sweetly for irony's
   sake
ha ha ha ha he's dying he's dying
   he's dead
a bloody fine time he
   picked
i haemorrhage over the hard wooden
   pew
the queen is at a party
andrew plays with koo

knowing the mind works against breasts

if you were a poet
i could have come
with simplicity of sky
but knowing
the mind works against breasts
i carry them sunless

to you skirting important talk
twisted wool plush
beneath my feet whispering
i'm on the pill
wanting other words
ungarbled unthick

freedom of dying
mennonite bones collapsing
into the springs
of a horsewoman's body
(that knew at twelve
the horse's naked spine's
effect

cowboy you've laughing eyes
hardness hotness probing
i split your back
with eagles' talons
down to the line
of cheek from cheek
clamp my lips on

the wanting words)
the sparse & unfamiliar neck
between thighs
that have ridden many horses
many miles
it is too soon
forever the last year
the hymen has grown again

my face rubs your stubble
scouring the last freckle
of self-preservation
like riding a bicycle
you never forget)
needing words traditional
silent cowboy
i might have said *hello*

you're the first

Grandfather Poetker

grandpa came from russia
in '24
his toes tapping in rhythm
to solemn shadows

if he dreamt on hot summer nights
of moonlight
& poetry no one could say
at his funeral

old men with red & rheumy eyes
spoke
of their fathers' heads toppling
like trees

in red forest dreams with surgical
precision

the other woman

you come quicker this time
for all your silver-weddinged years
have taught you

i want you   you say
as if i were a house   coveted

& i a proud & empty woman
unfold my legs
like a lawn chair

you settle in

i sigh

She Was Beautiful Then, Dancing

(in memory of Eva Fehr Klippenstein)

what is this thing she left him
for,   having painted the small room
yellow   splashing it with murals
of dancing bears   & the thought
of her return

& why   if she was leaving
did she stop to laugh with her man
with her babe,   her boy-child
grasping her breast
with all the strength of life

that we would want to laugh
with her,   with her dancing
in the tunnel of her leaving
laughing, dancing

okay joe

blue nun & cheeseburgers
with onions heads
wedged under steering
wheel listen to the song
joe amazing grace you
make me beautiful
rain playing taps
on the roof elbow
on the horn look
& laugh joe 2 sharp
honks & the man climbing
out of the lake &
stopping to look in
the car (heads wedged under
steering wheel) our guts
shaking together
& the patrol car passing
cops looking
1 sharp honk & shove
the seat back joe listen
to the song

The Adulterers: Trying to Say Love

there's a stone
in her shoe & too many
mosquitoes around
(this is how
the adulterers meet)
you got another boyfriend
he says asking really
if she's sleeping
with anyone lots & lots
she says meaning look
what you're missing
reynolds julio iglesias
randy andy
they're all after her
& why not

he persists

don't you want a boyfriend
he says meaning how
many boyfriends how many
lovers what's serious
even

in love

you know this is a guy
who wants to check out
the competition

they talk typewriters
you type oh of course
you do your poems
did you learn in school
no she tells him
i know where to put
my fingers after that
it's a matter
of practice

his up-from-the-belly laugh
means *with whom*
but she ignores that
woman of mystery
before act ii

there's a lady in town
she says who works
at the cheese factory
everyone laughs at her
for sleeping with
her married boss

what the hell is that
supposed to mean
he says
knowing

The Rider

chafed (naked) legs
aching bum
the ballast

of the woman's thighs
straddling
the piebald mare
shaggy
(the piebald mare)

side/long the woman's
legs (naked) shouting
to make a song
to sing

the woman   blue jeans
shorn   mostly moon
(up from)
the naked legs
the piebald loping

for the song the song
primordial
where hair & sweat
conjugate
on the (naked) legs
shorn jeans

it's almost 100
degrees
in the shade
the old schrug's
too hot
to buck

the woman's gone
mad with song
her throat
washed
with heat
notes foaming
from her lips
soaring flecks
of scores
& scores
dribbling
down her chin

madrigal of sweat
& hair (that is to say
the woman   legs a wreath
piebald mare)

rank sweat
(woman piebald)
make a song to make
a song singing

the piebald mare
the woman
the woman on the piebald mare
the woman's naked
lucid legs
riding

her shorts are
too small
her buttocks
slap
into the sweat
a line
of white flesh
surprised

out of her cut-offs
but what the hell
let the woman
be she's
happy

Gramma
(for Grandmother Poetker)

he's gone   every particle of him
husband father grandfather
words echoing through
his empty head
look he's dying
look he's dying

look outside gramma
how suitable the rain is
how basic our bewilderment
blue skies like the country song
blue eyes crying
in the rain

christ christ

tell me the difference
gramma between the curse
& the prayer
what are the holy places
now where can my feet
walk naked & innocent
while death pours into our hands
with the hard length
of his fame

no

my metaphor mistaken
the hand has no mouth
to swallow
all this at once

gramma you're not listening
to me shut up about
the *old* farm
off the road to steinbach
by friesen's peter
where the grass was greener
& the birds sang sweeter

gramma gramma
we got screwed

i say it louder & louder
but then knowing the rules
leave tears to mark
the pages

of worn german songs

A Friend Asks If He's Told Me He Loves Me

It doesn't matter how
you approach the door.
The house is blessed
with thick walls—
vines have made the great leap
of their kind
attaching themselves to the stone
below the doved roof.
It is a kind of faith
in the old house.
A home can be made.
In it birds have made their nests
& raised generations
as long as the *begats*
of the Bible
catching the darkening summer
with mellow song
& spiders with their secret webs
have taken their place among
the other creatures of the dark.
The window of the bedroom
is framed with ivory lace curtains
& beyond that you can see
the mountains & the valleys
where the bare-assed pines
straddle hillocks.
Sheep can be left to run
on the lower slopes
cows on the flatlands
to make a living.
If it were a woman's course
the crumpled earth & woodsmoke
would have wound themselves
into a painting
for someone to feel

the smell of it
to buy
to hang in a home or an office
as a fierce & tranquil explosion
of innocence & medium.

How to Have an Abortion

the waiting room
is off the elevator
to the right
people's feet wait here
on the vinyl floor

they are small feet
feminine
with two pairs of larger feet
at opposite
ends of the room

you leave your name
and cash
but there is no use
pretending
you are here
joining the other feet

hooked under chairs
or crossed but quiet
like well-behaved children

when your name is called
you jerk
surprise in the slap
of your foot
on the floor

this is acceptable behaviour
in feet
this is the way it works
you understand without
ever having been here

Fathers' Day Poem

1.
it's saturday night in the country
i'm first at the door
i take the winnipeg free press
from j.j. friesen's boy
first dibs on the funnies

the cows have been milked
& the manure's been hauled
to the fields in the honey wagon
but though it's daylight saving
the birds have quieted
& the night moths
have quickened the slash
of their wings

half-way up the stairs
i turn around
dad's in the living room
i give him the paper

thank-you   he says

i go upstairs & cry
into my pillow
the feathers of grandma's chickens
choke the sound

2.
the posts of the cows' fence
sag like a farmer
on his combine at harvest time
but the wires are electric
still rigid in their keeping

the old holstein cow stumbles
drops heavily against the wire
even from here you can count
the stars in her head
& imagine
the fire in her eyeballs

always after there's the bite
of remembered pain

3.
the day grandpa died
onkel diedrich knocked
yasch's head against a tractor
& left him there
to wake alone at twilight
& make his way home across
a half-section of alfalfa
dizzy & stumbling

4.
father's day

what can i say
when you don't listen
or don't want to listen
or pretend not to listen
as you & your father & his
perpetually sinned against
storybook fathers

it is only that a dog kicked
comes back to lick the foot
you know or the folds
of a heart closing around
the murderer's knife

you say well let's discuss
it then steal my words
& shoot them
back into my face

5.
the day after grandpa died
onkel diedrich caught yasch
against the side of the barn
with a pitchfork

the marks stayed
on yasch's belly
for a long time
afterwards

6.
the man has been moulded
into a caricature of furrowed
earth (sharp greens
earthy greys & browns

the iciness of blue)

pressure makes diamonds
but breaks men
the harshness of no dreams
no illusions
are etched like past birthdays
on the flat bleakness
of his face

the man's seed once swam
to meet him
but grew weak against the current
& couldn't hug him
for the fear
speaking later to horse
as he to milch cows
the mouthful of retorts
thought of too late

7.
but cousin yasch understood
sure yasch understood
what grandpa did to his dad
dying like that

& when yasch shot his father's horse
the horse went quickly
he got him clean
through the head

215

(for Grandma Wiebe)

it's 215 now   they've moved her from 218
i walk in but must leave
when an lpn comes in wanting to take
a urine sample

in the hall   leaning against the doorjamb
i hear the nurse tell *grosmama*
i'll come back later   mrs wiebe
to wash your bottom   do you understand
mrs wiebe

as though it's she that's old & not
                                    her body

the nurse comes out & tells me
i can go back in now
na audrey voh yeht et met dei
grosmama asks

i tell her good & she warms my hands
in hers telling me i mustn't stay long
because she doesn't want me to get caught
in the snow storm

i tell *grosmama* the line in armin wiebe's book
about *himmelfahrt* being the day
when jesus goes to heaven & mennonites
go to winnipeg
& she laughs until she almost *fuschlucks* herself
en vieb dann noch
yes   but no relation

grosmama   i say   *grosmama*
but can't remember the low german word
for love

everything here is a poem

i

(when you were away love
he says to the poet
i held the smell you left me
twisted dreams
into your multi-coloured thighs
left my tongue lolling
in your womb
you cold-hearted bitch)

three people i asked today
the poet says
one an *eltesta* in the church
how to say love
in low german

but no matter
the rain still pats my window
flowers grow
the dog pisses on my tires

& men will always ask
about the big O
in one way
or another

ii

problems come from conversations
the poet says
not from contiguity of thighs

love does not fill ethiopian bellies
the great black night
is not made white   translucent
for all that music

(the poet is slightly pink)

iii
women stretch
to fit any organ   still
all music does not receive
the same applause

when the poet left
she cried
that her belly did not swell
with music
preceding her into every room

she plucked her empty breasts
into a high lonesome song
imagining the music man
a young old prophet
with her lover's pointed beard
sucking heavy blue-veined breasts
in cadence

to the choral rain

iv
tricky this
looking right through
the garbage can at st malo beach
the grass & trees
undulating
through the mesh of metal

o the trick of lying light
the poet says
right out-loud

everything here is a poem
he says

(the poet cannot redeem herself
in the light of a thousand suns
lets well enough alone
& calls it love)

The Notorious Other Woman

looks for her earring in his truck bum
   pointed skyward & it is
an ordinary label on her jeans her
   head knocks against the steering wheel
though she hasn't found it yet
   knocked out she lies her face
half-concealed by the seat & the shadows
   among the empty cigarette packs & other
articles of faith it is
   the surprised please of her body he likes
& calls it sunshine her
   face that is flushed between
the accelerator & the brake she
   has been looking for
so long
now

in the theatre

did you miss me   a sculptured whisper
holds the wanting in my name scribbled
across a payroll that had your name
splashed across it like a catholic
miracle i cant see the goddamn theatre
is dark wheres the exit
suppose there was a fire
did you miss me babe
havent told you about meadowlarks & poetry
lines *published* perjured myself earlier
when i said i didnt go to x-rated movies
all prim & proper   *honey*
woke up this morning making love to a pillow
sleep crammed between my legs writhed
in my office chair until the boss asked
why this peculiarity   *yeah*
maybe

conversation

i have a little problem i
get a little jealous sometimes
often jealousy is the product
of ignorance of not having been
born a poet an odd seed-child of
love the problem is a problem
i don't like you going to parties
without me & shall i have you come
with me & your wife
& ask you how your sore neck
is born of back-seat fucking
this odd seed-child i hope
we have a good time at the lake
next week my wife & i our
friends will be there & you can have
too much of a good thing why
are you going to this party who
are you going with you don't
even like parties your sign
is all over the place gawdammit
in kleefeld in steinbach in st
pierre & on the twelve
everywhere i look there's honey
for sale

well dont you

you love me dont you babe
he said well dont you
what could it mean (i said)
i love pizza white wine
& dont think trudeaus too bad
either i mean its relative
like twenty-three years ago
from june 15 i cant conceive
of having not existed
or think of god not being mennonite
or your wife not finding out
god he says i love you
why you theres kathy whos reasonable
about things & her legs dont
argue philosophy
shes old (i say) the age of your
wife thats why its my belly
your beard tickles with kisses
& dreams he touches the snap
on my calvins & from there its all
downhill & up till finally
we see *blame it on rio* & leave
blushing furiously having had
no idea what it was all about —

Austria: Looking through the *National Geographic*

1.
the man in the picture
off to the left
has grown a beard
from too little
time to shave
from too much work
in Alpbach

lines bleed across his face
bisect his forehead
from his cheeks
and one cheek
from the other
like the crevasses
in the mountains

he holds no stein of beer
a month from now, perhaps
when the *Fremde* come
with American dollars

the *Zigarette* has burned down
almost to his yellow fingers
soon now, very soon
he will have to put it out

2.
there are two other men
in the picture
their faces are younger
and a little softer

that one there
to the right of the main man
(the man on the left)
you know has tumbled his woman today
like a wind in alpine fields
or an avalanche
roaring

his stein of beer is empty
after this hand
he will shout for the waitress
to bring him another
one hand dealing out the cards
the other stealing a pinch
from rounded buttocks
that strut their wound
bouncing indignation
mingling with the pride
of their plumpness

3.
down the line the other man
(next to the man
on the right of the man
on the far left)
is a bus driver who works
for a neighbour now and then
spreading manure on the fields

his clothing flowers
with the sweet stink

he washes his hands later
in a porcelain basin
in the blue gabled house
of his elderly aunt

his strong white teeth
bite into the *Roggenbrot*
his beer, a necessary river
to wash it all down

his clothing changed
to a blue striped shirt
and blue-grey pants
he will go to the inn now
to play *Watten*
yes, like in this picture
the air, smoke signals
of men leaving the trace
of their being on the walls
their mark on the white spot
where the picture of Charles
the last Emperor
was removed just yesterday

they talk, laugh, *Gott im Himmel*
now and then
as the cards return to the pack
like the sheep the bus driver's son
will herd tomorrow

4.
the hand in the far right corner
stained the deep colour
of sheep piss
has entered the picture
like an afterthought
though you know
it isn't so
you know that's what he wants

no face, no name to call him by
to say: he is this
or
not this

he is the necessary enigma
but his words have marked
the air in the inn anyway
in his teasing of the one
who loved his wife
the one full of *Roggenbrot*

they do not know
that I am here
they do not know
except for the enigma
who knows everything
who left only his hand
to mock
and silent words
to fill the air

but I am here
I am here, waiting
he must put out his cigarette soon
he must
now
while I watch

or have his screaming hand
drop the cigarette
to the floor
his face bursting
into the picture
his eyes flickering
in the smoldering skin
where his hand has touched
and will touch again
skin pulling away like onion peel
edges curling toward the flame
like this page
like this picture

leaving

(for Grandma Wiebe)

mother to my mother
mother to my grandmother
we are beside ourselves
a trinity of one
here in room 205

grandfather paces his steps
in the hallway
to the old rule
of don't-step-on-the-cracks

she's wanted to leave him
so many times
but lost the reasons
in the years
each child another gold ring
to weigh her down
to the flat earth

> *maybe tonight she thought*
> *devils taunt gently*
> *meaning no ill*
> *blossoming artlessly as*
> *puppy love*

but she learned with the birth
of each red child
to look at him
without a twitching eye
knowing how the person
most likely
to murder you is a member
of the family

maybe tonight swingers masquerade
as lovers and quick clever
fingers bring volcanic
satisfaction shudders echoing
through the years

she's ripped one tube
from her nose
another from her arm
in her manacled dream
she cried   mama
mama   help me

grandfather wants to hear *life*
though the lump she makes
in the middle of the bed
she calls dying
she won't give tongue to it

whatever word she used before
for staying
she will use now
to console

the shadows spill
from her dark irises
exploring the composition
of ephemeral harmony

dancers arrested
in a slow turn

coma
(for Susie)

(you can't paint sadness
of course you can't
paint lines

        & lie them so/ against the canvas

        that it stays wet on your cheeks
        you can't paint the tickle
        in your ear when a tear rolls
        into it or the lump screwing
        the hell out of your tonsils

like you can paint a mare
spreading quivering cheeks
to the delirium
of loveless probing

        you can't paint forever
        though i've heard of a man
        who wrote a song so sad
        people could only watch
        the vowels explode

round
& long
& easy)

after our shifts at the hospital
we phone around
scraping together your pieces
of progress into the miracle

of a twitching eyelid
a spasm in the hand
an accelerated heartbeat

at the sound of a name

in one fantasy you left your wife

in one fantasy you left
your wife
& i bore your children
david stephen & leah
were exceptional children
you would have been
proud of them
prime minister scientist
& astronaut
children you did of course
in that fantasy
love more than hers
it is impossible to believe
you lived importantly
before me
but wanting to watch dallas
with you
doesn't necessarily mean
i want it at all
it doesn't mean it's love
that i left
behind the quietest possible
closing of a car door
a fairly solemn suitable face
blue eyes registering
a mild surprise at the way
you wouldn't let the leaving
be clean & simple
without an autopsy
of the various flaws
in my character
it doesn't mean i loved you
that i cried by myself later
as a child does
lost in the woods

you know they're taught
by boy scouts or something
(the lost children)
to cling to a tree
& talk to it
like a mother

Susie

when grandpa died
i couldn't touch him
for the fear cramping
both sides of my belly
but though your hands are
cold in the coffin

i hold them anyway

they are not as cold
as i might have
thought them
before i got used
to death

i'm glad they got
your make-up right
your favourite blue shadow
on your eyelids
mary kay lipstick
on your mouth

the sun shines through
the clouds at the gravesite
i want to keep you here

open

so you can tan your body brown
warm as earth

summer always

your forehead doesn't furrow
when i cup your face
but my hands are warm
if i hold you long enough
you might make it yet

i won't cry

i won't beat my head
against a wall
pound my breasts through
thin skin
to my ribcage
or throw myself
on the coffin
in a spasm of grief

after the funeral
i'll call you
we'll talk of lovers
husbands & children
agree to meet for coffee
tomorrow

& say goodbye

A Poem for Michael: Lost in the Triangle

You've seen him, Big Empty.
Three times he came for you,
watched you in your head
and left. And still you say
he'll come back for you
and take you,
loving your every manic thought.
How you dream, while my silence
is its own consent,
having seen Big Empty myself
though not the mother-part,
thinking *this fellow is going*
to screw me until the flesh
melts off my bones and freezes
the blood of my pen.
Big Empty is a mirror, Michael,
with no colours;
the animals there, dirges.
Hands, thighs, breasts are all invisible
in that country
and are wrapped in dreams that leave
no air to breathe.
You can't make love in the houses there;
the floors are boards so soft
they could be the bodies of dreamers
from the way they give
with no groan.
There are only silent people there,
Michael, for all that the skeletons
dance for the worms of God
and forgive.
Which animal would I be for you, Michael?
Which face would you have me choose
in the morning after of one love
to another?

Still, the head is its own hell,
my silence louder than a yes to anything
to your dream of drifting
around in the Bermuda Triangle
growing brown,
brown like the quack-grass
in the drainage ditches back home,
the dream days of blue Bermuda
pressed into selective memory.
But I would find you
despite the darkness, like the animals
in my mythology.
I am the fair Hun here, growing fairer
in the unfamiliar sun
and brown; sun-dried hair on head
and crotch, two bright patches
for you to find.
The waters roil their tentacles around
the black patches sported rakishly
on our hearts,
my poetry and your songs
discovered on this boat one day,
in this sea somewhere.
There is no evidence of violence here.
There could be the embryo of a whimper
here but there is no evidence.
We have become our own mythology
and even twisted it into
a certain logic.
We have gone missing in the Bermuda Triangle.
Your Big Empty isn't empty, Michael.
You had thought he would be like vampires,
his reflection, no reflection.
Now you see his other face.
There are water spouts and hurricanes

in the Bermuda Triangle.
There are pirates and sharks
and the overwhelming notion
to throw one's self into the sea.
We are getting screwed here, Michael.
The head is hell.

so you say you love me eh

so let's pretend
for one minute
that you're human
(no three you say
most men last one)
from old pick-up trucks
on country roads

with nothing to do
but drink beer & swear
the northern lights
are trying to say something

(it may well be
a message from mars
mars men mars code)

as though smoking my cigarettes
were not enough
for murdered nerves
you twirl your chain cross
around your finger
faster & faster

now cross move again
a blur that catches firelight
& then you don't

love explain yourself

all things being equal
is a lie so let's pretend
only men suffer
& that the animals at the zoo
aren't all on grass
& that you don't supply
the mortar for the bricks
of the wall
the crux of it all
is knowing yourself to death

my love

alpha & omega

(for Mike — who didn't catch what I was saying)

we sat there
our words flushed
out no geese
for the hunter

we did not float
parachutes or drop
like stones
to ripple out

phrases of love
or of hate
we did not explode
into a spasm

of fragmented words
we did not implode
either there was
no fallout

of tongue or thought
it had nothing to do
with books
or thoughts

or whether
you actually can
hold out longer
than the average man

it had nothing to do
with poetry
there were
no land mines

mike loved i loved
we loved night
(in all its black
a certain light)
& how we plowed
our life into
a wooden floor's
beatitude we left
the splinters
as they were
& strung throughout
our pubic hair
all the candles
we could bear
we mowed & mowed
our rows of books
into the blue norther
coming through
into the reamed
forgetting earth
with children
ghosting in the dirt
we drove our herds
of sacred cows
into the realms
of thens
& nows
& lookit how
the temple filled
with holy men
the burning bush
then leaning out
the window frame
we pressed our guts

but it was
a killing ground
all the same
where we sat

only just recognizing
our witch of endor
our separate griefs
chalked on

the wooden floor
& in the centre
the goat's head
grimacing

hard into pain
& watched
the wafer in the sky
transform itself
to flesh
& die
in the winter
of our faces
we stumbled from
the holy place
& bent our backs
into the ground
of what we were
& what we found

The National News Had No Flashback on Your Life

yesterday i went to steinbach for a drink the
night sky was peculiar bloody in the south set
like a door in the star-scarred night it confused
me all of a while 'til the road broke through
& i saw the fall fires in the fields in the north
they didn't reflect at all the northern
lights splashed like semen across the stars the
bright one there i suppose the north the morning
evening star

Es erglaenzt uns von ferne
ein Land,
unser Glaubensaug' kann
es wohl sehn
und von Jesu gefuehrt
an der Hand,
wird sein Volk
dort in Frieden
eingehn

i look for you
everywhere
like an amputated arm
you feel itching
for years
in the dream
they say i followed
your coffin

i crept like a thief
into your bedroom
looked under the bed
in the closet
you should have
left directions

where are you susie

when i sing now
i sing in german

Laughter

(in memory of Grandma & Grandpa Wiebe)

22% interest on 38
hundred dollars
for the car grandpa
dievel deivel dunna
& schinda
but it serves me rite
you say stuff
that pride & get
a co-signer

na grospapa

which *zeed* does it
come from
vieb odah petjah

you have to laugh
i have to laugh
at your laughing
gramma look at her
laugh hand over
mouth thin shoulders
pressed forward
as tho to keep
the laugh for
emma und emma
we'll laugh
grosmama grospapa
me und gott
laughter ourselves

i sing for all my dead
in german

what you see

droning on in a monotone
like a bored bee
the teacher speaks
of little specks
on a piece of paper

the system has brainwashed
her into believing
that they are
countries

she is wrong
this is the greatest
stunt ever pulled
the secret that
the 11 o'clock news
is the longest
running
comedy in the history
of the electronic age

there is no england or france
or spain or the soviet union
or china
it is only a game invented
to keep students occupied
and adults glued to the t.v. set

there are no starving children
look about you   do you
see a starving child
i am telling you if it were
true the people would
never stand for it

The Night Is Thick & Black & Hot

i
the stones are sharp
to my bare feet
dad's old blue shirt spotted
with paint
(red   from the barn   white
the house) waves loosely
with the night

the night is black   still
for all that moon
but there's no fear in summer
not like in the fall
when you run from the barn
to the house
as quickly as you can
your shadow trembling
beside you

summer nights are thick
with dust   hot
with purpling lilacs
the smells of crickets   frogs
ripening wheat
in your nostrils

brown arms   legs
belong in the night
are one
with the night

the night is their lover

ii
the mare is a phantom
in the moonlight
she blows   softly
butts her head against my breast
the sugar i give her
she takes with delicate teeth
her smell thick

she stands   legs spread apart
tail hitched to one side
letting loose the yellow stream
i climb on her
her hair chafing my nakedness
her sides hot
like the night
like the songs cowboys sing
of creaking bones
& tolerable days

head low   she grazes
walks the night
i lean back
head on her broad buttocks
answer her blowing
with my own

Sisters
(for Karen)

1.
there is a magic in childhood
you'd just better believe it
my sister is suddenly
a six-year-old bayonet
she burrows into my breasts
to the main artery
and blood swells
the muscles of my throat
growling out an old sound
an old song

oh babylein

2.
there's a deep black hole
inside of her
like I used to hurt
she's hurting
but my youngest sister
is smarter than I ever was
she doesn't say it
she says it's a cold
so what am I supposed
to tell her

I give her two aspirin

3.
she pulls away
my breasts are useless
my musky smell
is not enough for comfort
and I'm not mother
I'm not big enough

4.
there's a deep black hole
inside of her
like I used to hurt
she's hurting
the song chokes to a halt
it is so old that I can't
remember the words
and my eyes are bloodshot
my fingers taste the salt
on my cheeks

a cold   I tell her

i had not meant not to play the game

i had meant   a leisurely
civilized evening
with some wine
the lamp

a gentle sort of shroud
a proper
emotional balance

that would not have
a silence
split in half
(an expletive

in god's mouth)

i had meant maybe
some intelligent
conversation
a building up

of all kinds
of clever defenses
& then a stretch

tummy in
my breasts the only valid
point to make

i had not meant
to take your face
in mine
to give

the crimson dream
a name
(bouncing grandchildren
on age-worn knees)

i had not meant
the thought
a sudden sweet
to call it meat

(making me horny
& birthing a poem
to speak as any christ
my god)

call it what you want

they called it heart-broken the day the nerve end-
ings marched themselves into a sanitarium,
checked in

because of the echoes in the shape of the shell,
from the pulses in the head & the sounds
in the vicinity.

but that was the one when i was fourteen.
he was the one when i turned sixteen.
three days after

two weeks later i learned what a soul is for
& how it can be stretched on a rack,
legs spread wide, each one tied

to a past of wire that tears the flesh in strips
in time to songs like 'you're the one in a
million' for the going through fire

yet to come. screams turning whimpers
over the corners, over the ridiculous,
over the space of what's

actual.
then joseph said it wasn't love six years
later & called it passion & the other guy

a fucking idiot.
& then joseph opened doors for me
& left messages at work that said

'i love you, doll, & most beautiful
creature' & knowing what wild things do,
tied a silken tether around my neck

knowing wild things, that i'd follow
the sun if he didn't give it a tug now
& then when i ran off with the others

until i loved him enough to fall
asleep in the shelter of his eyes & let him
tell me my breasts are beautiful

& that there was no music until
he heard my name
& no eyes as green as the blue in mine

while i slipped it all off, love & tether,
but gently, to watch the sun rise in the east
& i say if i hadn't left now

i would have had to leave a long time ago
for one with a past i can live in,
an animal mating for life

because of the echoes in the shape of the shell,
from the pulses in the head & the sounds
in the vicinity.

(you've got to take chances in life, lily,
my boss's wife says. there are no guarantees.
i would never have thought i'd lose

my son, she says, as though she forgot him
along with the toothpaste at safeway
& then she cries anyway, still talking

about having to take chances.)

this is an accident

after I heard about the accident
I puked

grandmother/grandfather/susie
this is too much God

truck coming/car out of control
grandma struggles to see anything
with her greying brown eyes
grandpa's knuckles are white
against the steering wheel
they shine like bone
and susie pulls her son
from the front seat to the back
her grip on her baby breaks her legs

the screams are indecent

I almost miss the funeral
for all the puking

the corners of my bedroom
retreat and advance
the ceiling pushes down
my head is a weight I don't want
my heart   amputate it

it comes down to clichés

but in the dream I took you home
(all of you   my dead)
on the train
snatched you right out of the graveyard
there are too many dead in that place
I want to talk to you
where I can scream
without those strangers' ghosts
looking on   denying me

this singular grief

& this is all

i will love you thru the harvest moon thru
the waning & the waxing
& will feast

on the fullness in my womb pull it thru
the thrust of my mouth
between teeth freshly brushed

& gently out i hold the coupling in my hand
& pray for it two nights a week
i will hold your skeleton in my

arms & pat
your shining head with loving memories
& a porcelain scream

this is a blue animal youre reading about

this is a blue animal youre reading about
but if you cant understand this or all
the rest ive shown you then there is no
understanding to understand this it is
a biblical beast a parable saving salvation
from the barbarians over & over again

it is a blue animal for all that you say
it is green reading this after the ones before
this is not what you had in mind of a love
poem of the three many words i cant show
you & let the blue animal live quietly
shaman let the blue animal live

would you have her stand blue naked
in a labial moment baring her soul to the hunter
you already possess more of the blue animals
soul than any god would ask this is not
an ethnic or dirty joke vulgar & obscene
you can put any definition on this as long
as its the right one & you dont ask

me to explain it is this a love poem you
wonder it doesnt rhyme the starry nights arent
here it is a blue animal youre reading about
not green but if you cant understand this or
the others then there is no understanding
to understand this is a love poem yes this is
a   love   poem   shaman

a love poem

touching home

sprinting along side of you
holding back against
the wind   letting you run
strong   head high
into the sweet summer
the grass is too high
field mice run & grasshoppers
pop like corn
down our path

& if you won
it was no sacrifice
but sacrament
in the days when you touching home
& me touching you
meant safe

susie is here
to complete our trinity
of youth   standing
on each others' shoulders
so high we see eternity
from the tire tied
to the old maple
by the lilac bushes

i remember brownie barking
the world tilting
at our laughter
at onkel john's laugh booming
out from the kitchen

now in your garden
of celestial calm
how infantile i must seem
to you   sister
writhing & genuflecting
at each lash of wind
but it's not so much
the words as that each
one finds a grief
to centre on
let's loose a string
of vowels around our necks
& speak of whales & seals
& how we liked to swing
when we were young
& in the raised crosses
& stone tablets
chisel the haiku

of our names

sunday evening

sunday evening   milking
dad's almost through   his face
as furrowed as his fields
in the fall   the *brumm*
of the 2550 john deere tractor
in his veins

the cows listen   shift
uneasily
at his summary
of the morning's sermon

the lone half-jersey heifer
among the holsteins doesn't kick
not today

across the yard the horses
magic & flyer twitch their ears
at the *dievel deivel dunna*
and *schinda*

silver grazes
chico grazes
her filly butting her udder

flies pile up around the barn
on the red rawleigh's
fly bait powder

one cat   no name even to call
it by in a mourning
stiffens   baring tiny teeth
to the wind

ronny pokes it with a stick
garry would mourn
but it's too late for a name
and the fascination of the maggots
in the corpse is too great

the cows mill out   slipping
stumbling   understanding a battle
unsure of their part in it
of the *plautdietsch* spoken
in the plain church down the road
with its practical windows

the bull   called milly
after an aunt
stares with opaque eyes
sweat gleams
muscles flow
in sheathed excitement

the sun   still hot   still high
in the sky takes cadmium light
from the fire on his flesh
from the eyes
god-wise enough to live
or die and never know
the difference

ronny tired of the game
takes the cat by the tail
(its got balls so it *is*
a boy) and throws it onto
the manure pile

tomorrow
it will fertilize the fields

Letter to Susie

there was a strange housekeeper
in your kitchen today
making cinnamon buns

but for that
it might have been
a rare dream
like a snow-covered field
underneath it all
you know there's rich
prairie dirt

growing dirt

you could sleep 'til spring
& the first meadowlark
all you'd need then
would be more clothes
parka   mittens
& you'd survive

sometimes we're best
at just surviving

the posts of the horses' fence
are sagging with the weight
of the early snow
last fall   if you remember
i tried to save the asters
in the garden
covering them with horse blankets
but they turned black
anyhow

they bled black

& a loneliness
got lost in them

Letter to Susie (ii)

when you were born susie
your mother's back arched
like a rainbow
until your father forced
her down afraid of the
splintering of bones
the winter sun
the eyes of stars
i use your name often
to give meaning to death
to the years it took us
to become friends
in between the loving
& the hating
i want to dig you up
right now
to touch your eyelid
& see if it comes off
in my hand
i want to see your bones
milked white by earth
teeth grinning
i want to use your skull
as a drinking cup
insert between your ribs
many red candles
for the christmas season
only carolyn listens
& helps me plan
to rob your grave
to bring you home
her dead brother's in california
she says
in the pictures

i've noticed how my friends
avoid me now
but they dream at night
of the world closing in
& of halley's comet
the once-in-a-lifetime
experience
last night i dreamt
that we were birds
white birds riding
warm currents of air
the night house-solid
around us the universe
pulsing

Letter to Susie (iii)

...for verily I say unto you, If ye have faith as a grain of mustard seed, ye shall say unto this mountain, Remove hence to yonder place; and it shall remove; and nothing shall be impossible unto you.
— Matthew 17:20

1.
today I picked up the pieces
of your life
a few bags of clothing
some make-up & jewelry

I love you
I can say it now
I love you

hide & seek's over
death freed me of that
& I a writer
can't control the story

the tear-wet hours

2.
we went to the mountains
the forest was thick
with reds & oranges
the mosaic of leaves
split earth
under our feet

there's an empty coke can
spearing the Queen Anne's Lace
dead fingers of wood
poke up through so many
years' growth of grass

looking up at those mountains
you can imagine
streams of rocks breeding slides
if you holler for an echo
you can imagine
mountains falling on each other
ridges sharp   cruel

no end to it

3.
the night air is cool
smelling of no season
& all this night
from dark to light
I have spent washing & ironing
those bags of clothes

I don't want them
not the pieces

you must know
I would have
if I could have
died instead of you
— not to cheat you of Heaven
but for your children

with their too-old eyes

4.
a firestorm blew
through the valley
leaving the trees blackened
on the south side

the trees
grotesque at night
claw into moonlight
glower

the survivors have
burn marks on them
but after the storm
they kept on growing

5.
the road that leads to the town
is an illustration
on vanishing points
in a book on perspective
where the mountains
come to water
motes dance
in eerie undulation
the water is stagnant
olive-green
lichen cling to mountain rock
the air is no thinner
of spiderwebs
& decay

6.
once we knelt to trace
the rings of trees
but that was far
from here—
one kneeling on
one sleeping in
flat prairie earth

sometimes seeing a maple
mottled red & orange
showing separate leaves
against the sky
I am consumed—
a fire of joy
a burning bush

then it all comes back

my eyes
seek your eyes
smiling eyes
sewed shut

next fall I'll plant
the mustard seed
but this is Manitoba dirt
there are no red-treed
mountains here to split
this separating earth
to eyes that see
& smile & weep
to echo back
my whispered

do you love

i remember going to calgary to read the day after her funeral no matter what anyone says   my mother insisting i go & throwing things into my suitcase & onkel peter & taunte leise bringing me to the airport   i don't remember reading but i must have done okay   i remember the trek down the 52 & the 206 from steinbach to silberfeld past telephone poles & empty cow pastures ringed with barbed wire & *no hunting* signs   i remember how my heels sank half an inch into the ground by her coffin next to grandma's & grandpa's grave   there was a pink & white & lilac wreath with a ribbon that said *wife;mother*   it didn't say *friend*   i sang real loud at the gravesite   i don't remember anyone else singing except for a man who might have been the funeral director if funeral directors sing

when we've been
there 10 thousand
years bright shining
as the sun
we've no less
days to sing
god's praise
than when we first
begun

when i followed her coffin down the aisle i walked real straight & i didn't cry   not then   not now   we've always been there for each other on important occasions   i helped her run away from home when she was sixteen   i was maid of honour at her wedding   i was there when her children were born & at her baptism   but they wouldn't let me hold her long enough at the grave to warm her up   when grandma & grandpa were buried three weeks before she was they sang *es geht nach haus*

you tired child
the roads are gold & clean
& sunny
wonderful sweet songs
banish your sorrow
we're going home
who knows   maybe
tomorrow

it reminds me of us sitting in church & taunte leise's alto rising above us all to float out at the very top of the tall skinny windows that usher neufeld unhooked to let the air in on hot summer days   sometimes we'd sneak outside in mid-service to breathe the scent of alfalfa flowers & trace the names chiselled on the gravestones of the mysterious dead   country earth takes a long time to settle in graves even as kids we knew that just because there was a pile of dirt on a grave it didn't mean it was fresh

die glaeubig flehn mit
traenen saen
sie sind im herrn
geborgen
ins heim so traut
das gott gebaut
ziehn wir
vielleicht
schon morgen

that's what they sang *es geht nach haus* the ground's real wet now but it was wetter then elvina's tulips are coming up i noticed them today when i went to the post office there's potting soil under my fingernails sweet peas morning glories larkspur phlox there will be flowers for the graves this summer but it's not yet a year too soon for bad verse in the back pages of newspapers really bad verse *in memoriam* loewen (wiebe) in loving memory of

in life i loved you dearly
in death i love you still
i know you walk beside me
& when my life is through
i pray that god will take
my hand & lead me
straight to you

lovingly remembered & sadly missed my feet writing the story over & over again my writing feet carrying me away from her past telephone poles & cow pastures barbed wire & *no hunting* signs from the first moment of grief to the song always singing in german always singing the prayer

gehe nicht vorbei
o heiland hoer
des herzens
schrei
da du andern gnad'
erzeigest
gehe nicht vorbei

Recent Publications from Turnstone Press

People of the Interlake by Andrew Blicq & Ken Gigliotti

Bloody Jack by Dennis Cooley

The Magic Trumpet by Victor Cowie & Victor Davies

Surviving the Paraphrase by Frank Davey

Grasshopper by Helen Hawley

mr spock do you read me? by Mary Horodyski

Thin Poems by James Hutchison

Seed Catalogue by Robert Kroetsch

Backing into Heaven by Steve Noyes

The Best Possible Face: L.B. Foote's Winnipeg by Douglas Smith & Michael Olito

No Fixed Admission by Jacqui Smyth

Headframe: by Birk Sproxton

Trace: Prairie Writers on Writing. Ed. Birk Sproxton

The Cartier Street Contract by Wayne Tefs

Waiting for Saskatchewan by Fred Wah

After the Revolution by John Weier